GILG

C000069764

A Collection of Haikus & Poems

By Dale M. Chatwin

A Kvasir's Blood Publication ©

Kvasir's blood was mingled with honey, thence was made the mead of poetry

This is a work of fiction. Names, characters, businesses, places, events, locales, and incidents are either the products of the author's imagination or used in a fictitious manner. Any resemblance to actual persons, living or dead, or actual events is purely coincidental.

Printed by Amazon Kindle Direct Publishing for

Kvasir's Blood Publications

ISBN: 9798852667458

Front Cover Design "The Womb" by Dale M. Chatwin ©2023
Author Photograph by Kate Ryan ©2023
Edited by Alice Bezant ©2023

kvasirsbloodpublications@gmail.com

Dedicated to

David Chatwin

1965-2023

Contents

Another Fading Lullaby

Fading lullabies,
Into the dead of night, I say goodbye,
Haunting melodies
I will leave behind when I die.

See the envy of the storm
Vanquishing with rapturous lamentation
I will breathe in anticipation
Upon the gears of my redemption.

The distant squall has left me blind
To the ones I love left behind
I lost my nerve upon oceans of time
Those stories in my mind
Are another fading lullaby

See the envy of the storm
Vanquishing with rapturous lamentation
Here I scream in anticipation

Within the cogs of my imagination

The Fates have tangled me in their grim threads,
My past and my future are newlywed
Beyond that veil I will wait and dread
There's a path toward home I long to tread.

See the envy of the storm
Vanquishing with rapturous lamentation
I cry once more in anticipation
For the day of my amniotic ascension.

Haiku Ϝ

Snow from my window
A memory fading fast
My vision fades too

Scattered Ruins

The girth of nature's bark bursts through
My bones beneath the fertile soil
While a lonesome lark toils a grim tune
To another stark morn, an alarm for the dead.

A forlorn soul am I who lingers
Betwixt leaves in mischievous sin
Fated to wander these acres
Without the skin of my life,
An ethereal blur.

My name is a number, etched into iron
Another fool of five thousand lives
Leaping for freedom, none of us surviving
No more will these cadavers stir
Only moulder and strive to be at one with the earth.

The metal of me, this cross-shaped effigy

Rusts into obscurity by the ebb and rise
Of Time's decaying tide,
Did I honestly believe you would stand there and cry?

Here, below this land, we are the scattered ruins
Of a forgotten memory, outcasts of society
Our energy of misery taints the air
With suffocating potency.

Yet, within the conquering plant life
A part of me, of us, will always remain
Bound to this realm with no shame
Reaching with limbs on the wind
A cold knife that cuts into your consciousness.

Our memories are restless
Our stories are timeless
They emerge, a new foetus
In a cycle of existential foolishness.

Earthly Insanity: Redux

I don't want to be here,
Where my sanity mutates into
Blooming flowers of madness
Where I become a malleable piece of putty
At the mercy of malignant hands
While my mind and body encompass
A creeping despair I cannot command.

I'd rather my soul glide
Into the embrace of the Grim Reaper,
Binding my soul to his forever,
Instead, I suffer with the colours
And agonising cries I try so hard to hide.

Don't make me go there,
Where my fears evolve into hideous stars
And I walk hand in hand with Fate,
A romance that takes us afar

Lost in a suffocating space
All memory of me gone without a trace.

I'd rather crawl inside my mind,
Where the heart cannot find me
Cowering in fear, a filthy lesson in voyeurism,
How I wish to be free from this colourful prison,
A prism of fury swelling inside my decaying body.

I want to be placed in an urn,
So the rainbow cannot haunt me
Or else I'll linger as an oddity,
A redux of a rumour unhappily spread
Through sympathetic emotions,
Eyes of heathens refusing to see me,
Dancing alone inside my earthly insanity.

Haiku ♭

Love, a word that binds

Mysterious to me here

In bed with my love

Yew Trees

Yew trees, vein-like branches caressing the sky
Weeping foam while rain soaks their blood-red bark
The earthy aromas bleeding from the dark earth
Leaves scattered like fallen warriors
Picked up by a breeze, nature's Valkyrie

Your blood spilled, absorbed by autumn
As a maelstrom of decaying debris
Swirled around your diminishing body
Carried by the yew trees to the sacred place
A sacrifice to soil, to worms, to the belly of the world.

The clouds moved across the vault in a procession
A celestial audience. Do the gods bear witness
To your gradual regression?
A house of stones, a house of limbs
A home for your bones where the hidden ones live

Runes marked your rest, a history buried
Soon to be dust
A memory seeping,
        trickling
Into each generation progressing after you
Through those woven threads
The web of your wyrd
Threads severed and lost.

While the yew trees wept foam
And you roamed smeared with death
The clouds faded,
        the procession receded
Your essence ascended,
        spiritual osmosis,
Beyond the Membrane
To begin anew upon another plane
Hearing your final breath.

Haiku k

Broken horizon
The sky filled with honeyed light
Healed spirit awakes

Haiku ᛗ

Angels peering down
Pillars of marble shroud life
Empty seats stare back

Haiku M

Falling stars marked her

Imperfections bring me love

Scars I long to kiss

The Seventh Rain

The seventh month
The seventh rain
Trickles through my trembling hands
Time leaks, life withers,
>   *A soul for a soul*
With grief I shiver

The seventh month
The seventh rain
Cruelly stings my aching hands
Fate grips, life is a blur,
>   *One cannot live unless the other one dies*
One mouth beckons the other one lies

The seventh month
The seventh rain
My hands try to catch it in vain
Time moves on, so do we all,

A vision throws us into Death's squall
My grief has become my conqueror.

Haiku ♪

Friends flock to the pier

Music flowing through our ears

My heart beats with love

The Day the Dead Sang

The old willow weeps
With lilted leaves
As ancient souls deceased
Slipped through the breeze
A choir of the dead
A crescendo of their lament

Fallen leaves drifted upon the river
To the ocean the water will deliver
The memory of the wind
From the day the dead sang
While the jackdaw chorus
In my living ears rang.

Haiku X

The looming lighthouse

An eye of radiance gazes

An echo of us

Mycobiota

The spruce-bark bled
Secreting its life
Clotting among the crevasses
Giving to me the strife of its death
I carved from it an infant creature
And laid it panting in the mulch
Engulfed in a viscous sheet
     Dripping.
     Yelping for help.
Clamouring for purpose
I abandoned it to nature's noose
So I could carve another

Fungal lifeforms flourish
Nourished by instinct
Chained to the earth
Until their girths swell
And these fruiting bodies

Ripened rip away from paradise

Shuffle towards hell

Tangible, yet hallucinogenic,

To cannibalise and sacrifice

Their plastic lives

Material lives

Disconnected lives

Vanity is their edelweiss

      Yet I was he who

      Carved them

      Laid them

      Abandoned them

So who is really to blame

For their addiction to fame

For their pursuit of digital validation

For their cosmetic ruination

For their morphological mutilation?

Who is to blame?

Haiku ᚺ

A star seeps through sludge

A cosmos of scum smothers

Ripples of time cease

The Gash

The gash of reality opens
     Like a wound
Pours light and colour
     Into the gloom

Suspended in our tension
     The bridge between our hearts
I am alone on the precipice of change
     My fragile being crumbles
At the thought of us being apart

Somewhere beneath the surface
     Our souls will be reunited
Somewhere a giant dies
     So that the small may live
Somewhere we will meet again
     In autumnal colours of youth
Underneath that painted sky

With raw magnificence

Our spirits gorge on love

                              In death we gorge on rebirth

To gorge ourselves on life

                              To return to the gorge of death.

Gilgul

The umbilical cord

Contains myriad movements

A slew of slaughter

Primitive procreation

Gestating in the unformed

Malnourished brain

Waiting to slither

From the fleshy drain

Once again

    It never ends

Gelatinous eyes jiggle

Quiver unblinking

Downloading energies bestial

A feral inhuman force

Uncivilised untaught

What came before

Doomed to repeat again

It never ends

Past teachings transude
From membranous tissue
Not to be absorbed
Never to slake our thirst
For fate, for ruin,
Flee to the fleshy dungeon
To do it all over again
　　　It never ends

Lackadaisical limbs gesticulate
Prodding the walls, desperate
Abort this travesty
This futuristic fanatic
This potential hazard
To humanity, to nature
To all creations we pretend to adore
On the amniotic shore it waits
To repeat ancestral mistakes
Returning to the womb again and again

It never ends

Yet Fate in its wisdom decrees
Birth this damned soul
Lost in its infancy
Lost in its past tragedy
Lost without a memory
Unable to learn
Formed only to yearn
For something unattainable
Love, friendship, family
A trinity never to be gained
The cycle consumes
The cycle retains
An imprint of our flaws
Again, and again
> *It never ends*
> *It never ends*
> *It never ends.*

Sequoia

Giants exist
Residing in our forests
Motionless you stand
Dominating England's quaint land

Your bark is like sasquatch fur
Yet no doubts of your existence stir
Your girth is a monster
Your birth a tall-tale
In your presence all things quail

      Fire cannot scorch you
      Insects cannot infest you
      An axe will never cleave you

Out of myths you came to our shore
Planting your roots into our lore
If I photograph you

Will the image be blurred?
To preserve your image, I would be honoured

A multitude of appendages
Hang from your herculean body
Prickling like the tail of the manticore
But you are gentle, like the herb-eating stegosaur

I look up to your citadel
Surrounded by nature's auditorium
My spongy brain dizzy and lustful
My hands touching your spongy bosom
Your existence I cannot fathom

Gently you absorb my mortal form
Sequoia, adorn my flesh with your tannin
From within your trunk I will be your sexton
My body infusing with this, my bohemian bastion
As sequoia grows beyond the reach of falcons
And inside her a new spirit awakens.

Boobrie

The craggy corners of this window
I peer through, a silent watcher,
Mesmerised by a strop of razorbills
Serenely seesawing upon the water

A cerebral portal
Into my traumatised past
On the isle of Tintagel
My fate is forecast

The razorbills

      Dip

Emerge

                           Flit

Towards the cliff

Stained with their shit

Does their presence herald a storm?

One perches on the portal before me
Could it really be?
A close encounter with this bird of the sea?

With a ruffle of feathers
The auk grows in size
Engulfing the portal with its blackened beak
Scrutinising my being with its curious eyes

"Resolution" it speaks to my heart
While fecund fish from its maw fart
"Resolution" I reply
Then I lay down and cry
Until the shroud of night

With a rumble of thunder
The boobrie takes flight

In the form of a moth

Towards the moonlight

On the cliffs the razorbills call

As the moon is marked once more

With the soul of another traveller

And I peer down on the earth

                    Forevermore

Haiku I

Leviathan fall

A barrow, but new life grows

Roots unearth my soul

A Creation Myth

In the beginning, there was the God of Six,
Known in a forgotten time
In a forgotten tongue
As Swéksōs.
There, within the petrifying realm of nothingness
Ruled by Derkaz,
It existed, a hexagonal entity that encompassed infinity.

After unfathomable years Swéksōs grew pregnant,
Eager to conquer Derkaz and end its
Reign of stifling void.
Within the womb of Swéksōs
There multiplied an untold number of
Gelatinous hexagons
Filled with oozing golden light.
For aeons they gestated,
Inside that cosmic amniotic sac,
A pulsating mass.

The Children of Swéksōs

Intricately intwined to form the Membrane.

Then, once fully designed,

The Membrane procreated with itself,

To vanquish Derkaz

And populate the nothingness with life,

Thus, fulfilling the will of Swéksōs.

Beneath that throbbing chrysalis

Began the articulation of infinite universes,

All partitioned and protected by the hexagonal veil

Which we have come to recognise as our progenitor,

For all things came from the Membrane,

And so, they shall return.

Haiku ✦

City of sirens

Their carrion roam dead here

Consumed by false hope

A Prayer to Rán

Hail, Lady of the Northern Seas,
Whose hair lies in all the waving weeds
In all the shoreline, each grain of sand.

Hear my prayer, hear my plead.

Hail, wife of Ægir, mother of the Nine,
Goddess of the salt waters,
Mother of plankton, mother of anemones.

Hear my prayer, hear my plead.

Hail, Lady who challenges us to see
That Nature is not under our control,
That we are only a small part of the world,
That we are flesh and flesh can drown.

Hear my prayer, hear my plead.

Hail, Mother of the Ocean
And may we come to appreciate your realm
Before you take it from us forever
Oh, Rán, aid us in our need.

Hear my prayer, hear my plead.

The Mid-thirties Blues

Four years from thirty,
Nearly five.
As a child, did I expect to be alive
At this age?

Wrong side of thirty
Gears clink monotonously,
Dopamine hit after dopamine hit
Time no longer exists,
The reality- check.

Stuck in the middle of thirty,
Delving into debt,
Every paycheque reflects
My job, the albatross around my neck.

To the young I am old,
To the old I am young.

Where do I belong?
Time cannot be prolonged.

Neither can age,
My friends and I are on the same page,
We rage at the future, long for the past,
Our lives in youth once seemed so vast,
Now we realise that nothing ever lasts.
Immortality was advertised,
We reached for that elusive prize,
Our ignorance was our own demise,
Our dreams were denied,
It was all a sleazy televised lie.

One day all things must die,
Grandparents die,
Parents die,
Friends die,
We too shall die,
And the next generation
Will learn the same truth,

And experience their own mid-thirties blues.

People Watching

Who are these faces
What are these mouths
Mouths and faces
Faces and mouths,
Sucking air
Expressing despair
Exhaling pollution
Earthly contusions.

Where do they go
These mouths and faces
Faces and mouths,
To and fro
Across the globe
Aimless journeys
Amaurotic bees
Lost without their queen
Trapped in their digital dreams.

Caught in the rain
These mouths and faces
Faces and mouths,
Under swollen clouds
Soggy rats
Sewer rats
Rat-a-tat-tat rattling
Emotions flattening
Gutter slick with scat
From washed-out aristocrats.

Innocuous sounds
From these mouths and faces
Faces and mouths,
They talk about nothing
Think they're saying everything
Mindless incantations
Excessive vocal masturbation
I am tired of their false rationalisations.

Perpetual gasses

From these mouths and faces

Faces and mouths,

Secreting anal mould

Excreting from unholy holes

Exhibiting their belligerent bowels

Together in their scandalous shoals

Destroying my soul

O my soul

My poor watchful soul.

When will I be free

Of these mouths and faces

Faces and mouths

House me in solitude

Hopeful of some fortitude

Who am I to delude

My mouth and face with this barren truth

Lonely truth

Sympathetic truth

Bullshit truth

I have no truth

I fear the truth.

The Fowl

The fowl flock
To the foul food
Discarded by humans
Who consume and spume
For their greasy gut garbage,
The fowl acknowledge
Ignorant.

An orgy of greed
Wasting their money
On vapid vittles
Here by the seashore
The fowl wait in hordes
Poised omens always wanting more.

Their innards are in ruins
The fowl splatter the shingle with shite
The hoggish humans caught in a riptide

Of faecal annihilation,

The fowl cackle as their victims flee and slip,

Woe betides beachgoers who buy fish and chips!

A Letter from My Dad

I found a letter after you died
Inked words that reverberated through time
You had sent it to me when I was ten
With statements I could not fully comprehend.

I do not know where to start.
The feeling is mutual
I have not the heart
To write this poem
But I will.

I have missed seeing you
The hardest thing I have ever done
Is walk away from you.
A father writes to his young tear-struck son.

I wasn't being the dad I should have been
I am not a nice person

And I hope you grow into a better man.
The pages are stained with fresh tears as I read.

Ashes, ashes, ashes,
Your body is ashes
Your blue eyes are ashes
Your chance to be a father is ashes.

I, like you, feel confused and lonely
Maybe the decision I made was the right one
But remember, you will always be my son.
All I feel now is sad and angry.

I saw you a week before you died
What happened in the past we need to put behind
The last words you spoke to me
As the cancer gnawed at your withering body,
And once again I'm left feeling confused and lonely.

It is not your fault
It is all down to me

I have only caused upset

The letter trembles and I ask the emptiness:

"Did you ever feel any regret?"

But only my tinnitus answers back.

We will meet again,

I am not sure when,

Be good to your mum,

Love, always, your Dad.

At your funeral I finally set you free

I will scatter your ashes into the Irish sea

And remember the father I so briefly had

Perhaps we will meet again upon some distant land.

Haiku ʃ

Personality

Filled with positivity,

Impeccably you.

Haiku ♈

Gross humidity
The city is desperate
I hold her closely

Cough Drops – A Nursery Rhyme

A bat flew into my grandad's shop,

'Cough drops, cough drops'

It shouted at him,

My grandad was silent,

No answer did he give,

He had cough dropped,

Cough dropped,

Of Covid-19!

Anniversary Poem

Our memories are streaks of ore
Trickling through time,
The cliffs carve our love
With veins of fossilised rhyme.

The past is a metamorphic act,
Viewed now as lyrical strata,
Erupting above, a colossal sequoia,
A shrine to our love.

As we lay beneath its roots
In a psychedelic pact,
We whisper, I love you,
A sober and simple fact.

Proem from The Whale of Wessex

Let us tell you of the Season of Madness,
Where the threads of our fates were conjoined
With a curse, from Urd's Well it came,
In Miðsphere it reigned
To reclaim the Vomitory stage.

Oh, Kvasir,
Allow us to sup on your mead of poetry,
So that we might find the words
To recite these grotesque events witnessed
By eyes that now wish to be blind.

Oh, Tīw,
Lend us the courage to purge
These gelatinous dreams,
Memories plaguing our souls,
Night upon night,
A flabby horror which inside our minds
Is a maddening blight.

Tell us, wise Wōden,

Which course we should take

When pen marries paper,

Help us to see wisdom through our madness,

Lest our sanity be lost forever,

Plunging us into darkness,

In this tale we tell of the Whale of Wessex.

A Letter to My Dad

Dear Dad,

Throughout my life there has been a vacuum

Left behind by you,

You rationalised your reasons

Expecting me to understand,

But I was a boy, far away from being a man.

Over years you came and went

Brief moments spent

Exploring the man who helped to create

The one that writes this letter in grief.

Demons haunted you,

Do they also haunt me?

Are the sins of the father inescapable,

Or can I break the cycle?

Can we ever truly be free?

Your decision to leave me on the doorstep

Left a stain on my being,
I cannot have children of my own
In fear that I too I will abandon them
And be just like you,
Inheriting your throne.

Before you died I saw you,
The tall imposing man of my childhood
Reduced to an emaciated husk,
Our exchanges were brief,
Just like our relationship,
I didn't know you would die the following week.

We all wish we had more time,
More time, more time,
I do.
More time to mend our broken hearts
To suture the wounds before you depart,
More time to talk about what the future holds,
More time to forgive before you grow cold.

Throughout my life there has been a vacuum
Left behind by you,
Now, with your death, the vacuum is closed,
For you cannot return from where you now roam.

I have learned to forgive,
It is a difficult journey,
Wading through anger and bitterness,
The sludge of hatred,
It becomes a burden to the soul,
So, Dad, I forgive you,
For what is done cannot be undone,
And so, we must move on,
Love, your Son.

A Grim End

Cold hard grotesque
The heart is a pustule
Pumping poison deathly substance
Oozing into capillaries
A foetid clog in the arteries
A stiff precipitation
Ejaculating from this aroused prison
A perpetual judgement
From perpetrators of reason

Who are they to finger the asshole
Of this perverse ringleader
Slackened jaw driblets of drool
They examine his stool
But find only a fool
Trapped by his own fate
Consumed by critters of hate
While he picks at the lock
Trying to open his heart

Produces naught
And plunges into emotional drought

Yet he drowns in the secretions of his stiff spout
A quivering coalescing stench
Shoving a pastry in his mouth
Not caring where it comes from
Florets of mould his eyes behold
A super sleuth of hygienic truth
Turned to a ruthless reckoning
From the ombudsman of Grim
Reaching with fingers scabbed and slim
This droll doll controlled by his bedlam

Under his skin transforms into a warped troll
Limping on his crutch of pain
With newfound purpose and gall
He runs for the nearest train
Head stuffed with a moral migraine
Feet flying over the rails with no shame
This smiling chanting antithesis of spirituality

Buys a one-way ticket

Casting his life into Grim's net in vain

Leaping into nothing.

Cause nothing is how it ends.

Haiku ✝

Trolls lurk in the rain
Their magic blots all I see
Runic pearls unfold

Haiku ⊏

The womb I escape
Will I remember the end?
Walking towards light

Sigewif

The land breathed,
Its grassy dunes lifted like lungs,
Then collapsed into the moment,
While Þhunor, growling,
Proceeded to sow electric seeds
Across the horizon of dead flat clouds,
His fury a shroud for the offering tongue.

You breathed,
Chest inflating and collapsing,
Symbiotic with the land,
As the battle chant, furious intent,
Rose to a crippling crescendo of silence,
A deep breath, a meditative balance,
Erupting in a dissonance of dread.

Your hair was dangling, sweat slick,
Moist snakes, venomous lick,
Shrieks high pitched,

The hand eagerly twitched,
Thorn-eyed woman of the army's sigewif.

The hand complied,
The spear was allowed to fly,
Death riding, hear Gungnir singing,
Your teeth mashing,
Fists bashing your bare breasts
In time to the shield wall smash,
The seax plunging into guts,
Turbulent waves of intestines,
Your beauty spattered with blood,
A maddening lotion.

Plundered rings adorned your arms,
As arrows, like bees, buzzed past your eyes,
The horde quailed in fright,
You shrieked into the night,
A pale bride to the Terrible One's delight,
While on your farm your children wait,
Orphans given to the bosom of Fate.

The women were swarms,

As the men cheered and roared alongside,

Unleashing their fury,

Þhunor smashed with pride,

Raw violence, the army charged to victory,

While you stood and smiled at your enemy's sufferance,

An orgy of heathens in endless crimson conflagration.

Our sigewif was bludgeoned,

While all the men hearkened to her death-song,

Howling like wolves at the darkened sky,

The cloud-filled chasm fissured,

A throng of swan-maidens descended,

Into the High Hall you were taken,

Passing away from memory into legend.

As you drifted,

You saw ravens feasting on your naked corpse,

Like you, those carrion birds felt no remorse.

Haiku R

The cycle repeats

Here on this realm I remain

Echoing mistakes

Author's Note

I would like to thank you, dear reader, for purchasing and reading this body of work. As you know, this collection is an independently published piece. I self-publish all my work as I feel this gives me total creative freedom. Because of this, I need all the support I can get in helping this work reach a wider audience and getting the recognition I believe it deserves. Purchasing this collection is the first stage of your support. The next stage is leaving a review. As an indie writer it is very difficult to get people to leave reviews, so I would be very grateful if you could head on to the website you purchased this novel from and leave a review, whether it be on Amazon or even Goodreads. It doesn't have to be a long review, just something to let me and other readers know what you think. Most importantly I want you to be honest.

Scan the code and discover more of my works

Printed in Great Britain
by Amazon

36336118R10046